MY WORLD OF SCIENCE

Magnets

Revised and Updated

Angela Royston

Heinemann Library
Chicago, Illinois

© 2001, 2008 Heinemann Library
a division of Pearson Inc.
Chicago, Illinois

Customer Service 888-454-2279
Visit our website at www.heinemannraintree.com

Designed by Joanna Hinton-Malivoire
Printed and bound in China by South China Printing Co. Ltd

12 11 10 09 08
10 9 8 7 6 5 4 3 2 1

New edition ISBN-13:   978-1-4329-1436-3 (hardcover)
                         978-1-4329-1458-5 (paperback)
       ISBN-10:   1-4329-1436-7 (hardcover)
                         1-4329-1458-8 (paperback)

The Library of Congress has cataloged the first edition as follows:
Royston, Angela
  Magnets. / Angela Royston
    p. cm – (My World of Science)
  Includes bibliographical references and index.
   ISBN 1-58810-243-2 (HC), 1-4034-0042-3 (Pbk)
   1. Magnets-Juvenile literature. 2. Magnetism-juvenile literature.
   [1. Magnets. 2. Magnetism.] I. Title.
   QC757.5 .R695 2001
   538'.4-dc21
                      00-012872

Acknowledgements
The publishers would like to thank the following for permission to reproduce photographs: © Photodisc p. **14**; © Powerstock Photo Library p.**15**; © Stockshot: p. **18**; © Trevor Clifford: pp. **4, 5, 6, 7, 8, 10, 11, 12, 13, 16, 17, 19, 20, 21, 22, 23, 24, 25, 26, 27, 28, 29**; © Trip p. **9** (M. Barlow).

Cover photograph reproduced with permission of © Alamy/Ace Stock Limited [Photolibrary].

The publishers would like to thank Jon Bliss for his assistance in the preparation of this book.

Every effort has been made to contact copyright holders of any material reproduced in this book. Any omissions will be rectified in subsequent printings if notice is given to the publishers.

Contents

Any words appearing in the text in bold, **like this**, are explained in the glossary.

What Is a Magnet?

A magnet is something that can pull some things toward it. The magnet has a **force** in it that you cannot see. You can only see what it does.

This fishing rod has a magnet tied to the end of the line. The magnet pulls the fish toward it. How many fish has the magnet picked up? (Answer on page 31.)

Magnetic or Nonmagnetic?

Magnets only work on some kinds of **materials**. If something is pulled towards a magnet, it is said to be **magnetic**. A metal paper clip is magnetic.

You can use a magnet to test whether
something is magnetic or nonmagnetic.
A magnet cannot lift a leaf, so the leaf is
nonmagnetic.

Magnetic Metals

Most metals are hard, strong, and shiny. There are many different metals. Not all metals are **magnetic**.

All these things are made of metal.

Iron and steel are metals that are magnetic. Iron and steel are used to make many things, including trains, bridges, and paper clips.

Shapes of Magnets

Magnets can be any shape. The most common shapes for magnets are a horseshoe and a bar.

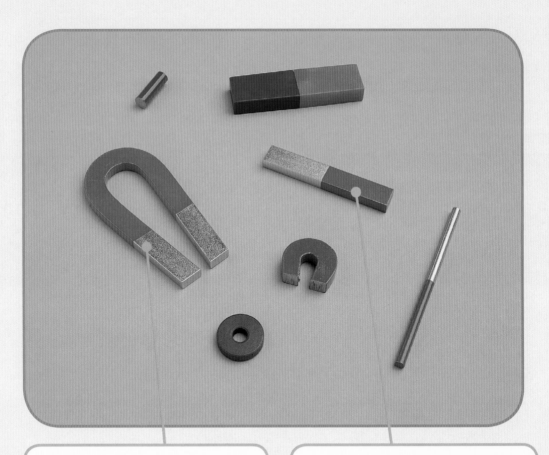

horseshoe magnet

bar magnet

The shapes that stick to a fridge have a small magnet on the back. The magnets stick to the door of the fridge because it is made of steel.

Test of Strength

This girl is testing which magnet is stronger. She puts a nail on a line on a piece of paper. Then she moves one magnet slowly towards the nail.

When the nail moves to the magnet, she marks where the magnet is. She does the same with other magnets. The strongest magnet pulls the nail the farthest.

Using Magnets

A **recycling center** uses magnets to separate aluminum cans from steel cans. Only the steel cans are **attracted** to the magnets.

magnet

crane

Magnets are used to move heavy loads of metal. This crane has a huge magnet on the end. It can lift and move metal that is too heavy for people to move.

Magnets at Home

Knives can stick to a **magnetic** knife-holder. What metal do you think the knives are made of? (Answer on page 31.)

rubber strip

The door of a refrigerator has a rubber strip covering a magnet. The magnet under the rubber pulls the door closed. The rubber strip **seals** the door to keep the cold air in the refrigerator.

Compasses

A **compass** uses a magnet to tell you what direction you are going. The compass needle always points north. Hikers and sailors use compasses to find their way.

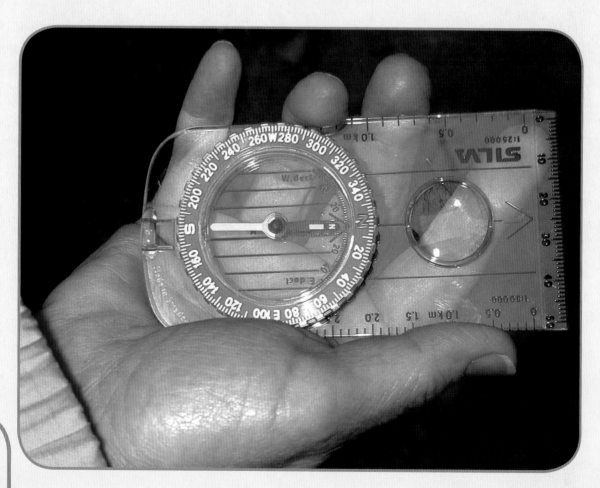

This is a home-made compass. It floats and can turn on the water. One end of the magnet points north and the other end points south.

Magnetic Poles

This magnet was placed on top of a pile of pins. The strongest parts of the magnet pick up the most pins. Which is stronger —the ends or the middle? (Answer on page 31.)

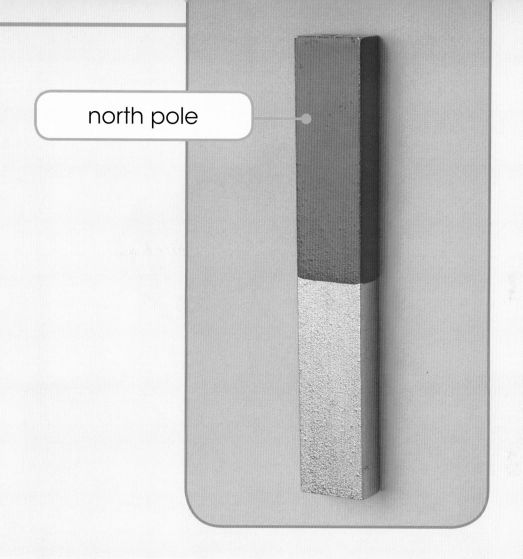

north pole

The ends of a magnet are called the poles. One end is called the north pole and the other end is called the south pole.

Poles that Attract

north pole

south pole

The two poles of a magnet are not the same. The north pole of one magnet **attracts** the south pole of another magnet.

You can feel the poles pulling towards each other. The attraction is very strong. Sometimes it can be hard to pull the magnets apart!

Poles that Push Each Other Away

Sometimes magnets **repel** each other. You cannot make a north pole stick to another north pole. They push each other away. Two south poles also repel each other.

These magnets are floating above each other. The poles are at the top surface and bottom surface of the ring magnets. They are pushing each other away.

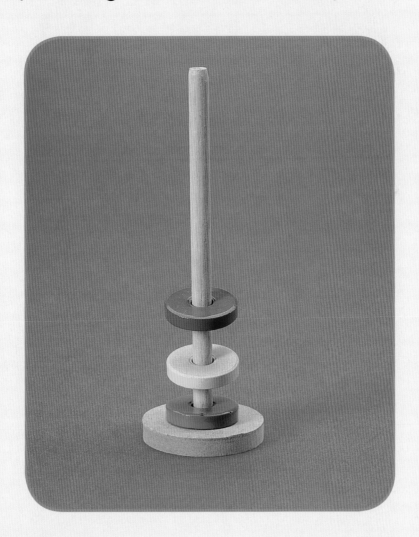

Magnetized!

When iron or steel sticks to a magnet, it becomes magnetized. This means it becomes a magnet too. The first paper clip magnetizes the second paper clip.

The stronger the magnet, the longer the chain of paper clips. But if you remove the magnet, the chain falls apart. The paper clips are no longer magnetized.

Making a Magnet

You can make a magnet that lasts. This boy is stroking a nail with a magnet. He strokes it about 50 times, in the same direction.

The nail becomes a magnet. It is strong
enough to pick up a paper clip. You can
use one magnet to make lots of other
magnets.

Glossary

attract pull towards something

compass tool that uses a magnet to tell you which direction you are going

force power that makes things move

magnetic something that can be pulled towards a magnet

material what something is made of

recycling center place where used glass, metal, and other things are collected to be made into new things

repel push away from something

seal to close something so tightly that nothing can get in or out of it

Answers

Page 5—The magnet has picked up two fish.

Page 16—The knives are made of steel.

Page 20—The ends of the magnet are stronger.

More Books to Read

Riley, Peter D. *Everyday Science: Magnets.* Strongsville, OH: Gareth Stevens, 2002.

Sadler, Wendy. *Magnets: Sticking Together!.* Chicago: Raintree, 2005.

Index